ROYALS HOLD GRUDGES FOR 100 YEARS!

The Hundred Years War
History Books for Kids
Chidren's European History

BABY PROFESSOR
EDUCATION KIDS

Speedy Publishing LLC

40 E. Main St. #1156

Newark, DE 19711

www.speedypublishing.com

Copyright 2017

How could a war go on for a hundred years? What was it all about, and who won? Learn what England and France were fighting about during the Hundred Years War!

THE NAME OF THE WAR IS WRONG!

The first thing we should know is that, while England and France fought each other over a very long time, it was not a single war. In fact, there were periods of peace between the countries that sometimes lasted several years.

Battle of Waterloo

The second thing that is wrong with the name is that the conflict between England and France lasted for more than a hundred years. This particular set of wars started in 1337 and went on until 1453: 116 years.

In a larger sense, hostility between the two countries could be said to have gone on for almost a thousand years. William of Normandy, a French subject, conquered England in 1066 and became its king. But, as Duke of Normandy in France, he continued to be the most powerful vassal, or subject, of the French king. So England was a separate nation while its king was, in some ways, under the king of France, a different country. This caused strains for hundreds of years.

William the Conqueror

Siege of Sebastopol

France and England fought each other in almost every century after 1066 until 1904, when the two countries signed pacts of friendship called the Entente Cordiale. They had also sometimes been allies over those years, as when they fought on the same side in the Crimean War from 1853 to 1856.

A WAR OVER TERRITORY AND THE THRONE

The fighting in the fourteenth century came about for two reasons, control of a part of France and the question of who would be king.

Crimean War

Bressuire

Châtellerault

Parthenay

Poitiers

**DEUX
SEVRES**

VIENNE

Montmorillon

Niort

Bellac

Guéret

CREUSE

HAUTE

La Rochelle

St-Jean-
d'Angély

Confolens

Aubusson

Limoges

Rochefort

CHARENTE

Rochechouart

VIENNE

Saintes

Angoulême

Ussel

Cognac

MARITIME CHARENTE

Nontron

CORREZE

Jonzac

Tulle

Périgueux

Lesparre-
Médoc

Brive-la-
Gaillarde

Blaye

DORDOGNE

Libourne

Bergerac

Bordeaux

Sarlat-la-
Canéda

GIRONDE

Arcachon

Marmande

Langon

Villeneuve-
sur-Lot

**LOT ET
GARONNE**

Agen

LANDES

Nérac

Mont-de-
Marsan

Dax

Bayonne

**PYRENEES
ATLANTIQUES**

Pau

Oloron-
Ste-Marie

Aquitaine

In the fourteenth century the duchy of Guyenne, or Aquitaine, had been owned by the kings of England since 1135, but was held as a fief, or dependent territory, from the king of France. When King Edward III of England gave refuge to an enemy of Philip VI of France, Philip took over Aquitaine in 1337. England went to war to get back territory it had held for two hundred years.

The second issue was who should be king of France. When Charles IV died in 1328, the person with the best claim to the throne was the king of England. The French nobility hated the idea of an English king, so they changed the rules of inheritance to disqualify the king of England. Once the war started in 1337, England's King Edward III revived his claim to the French throne.

King Edward III

Battle of Trafalgar

ENGLAND MAKING GAINS

At the time France was the most powerful nation in western Europe and had a much bigger population than England's. However, England was able to send trained, disciplined armies into France to defeat much larger French forces. The English used archers with longbows to defeat the French cavalry and infantry from a distance, and won remarkable battles against long odds. England also had great success over France in battles at sea. Here are some highlights:

SLUYS – 1340

The English fleet destroyed the French fleet in a sea battle, giving England control over the English Channel for the rest of the conflict.

CRECY – 1346

The French had a much larger force in this battle, and the English were far from their source of supplies, But the English archers handed a huge victory to their army.

Battle of Sluys

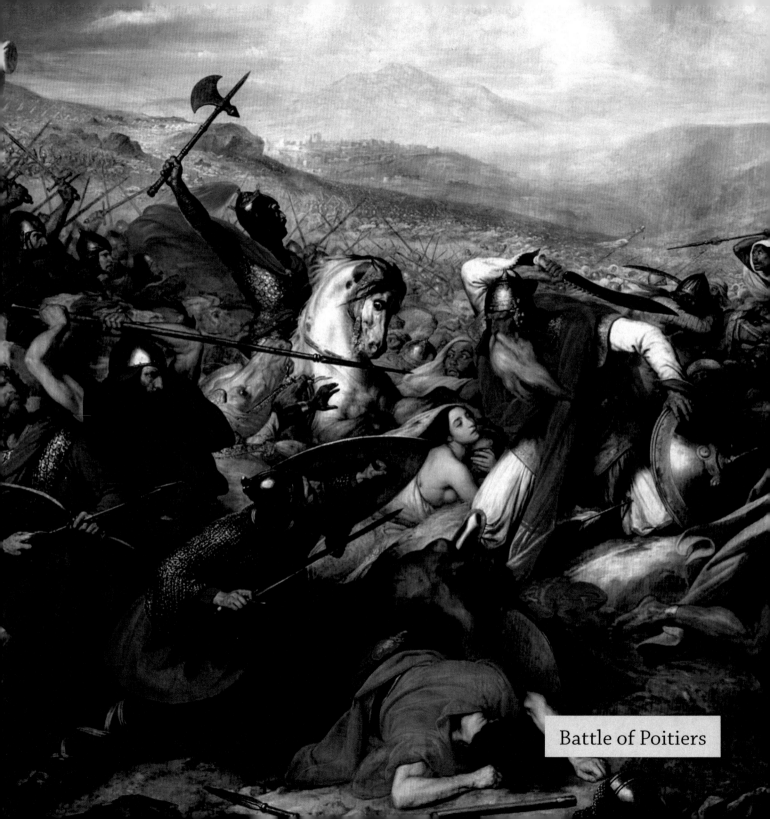

Battle of Poitiers

POITIERS – 1356

The much smaller English army tricked the French into attacking before they were ready. The English archers destroyed the French cavalry by shooting their horses out from under them. King John II of France was captured in this battle.

In order to save his throne, King John agreed to a treaty in 1360 that granted independence from the French king to Aquitaine, and enlarged it so it covered almost a third of France. In return, the English king renounced his claim to the throne of France. France also agreed to pay millions of pounds of ransom money to England for the release of their king.

King John II of France

Peasants' Revolt

CAPTURE THE THRONE!

The peace ended in 1369, and slowly France regained most of the territory it had ceded to England. England was distracted by wars with Scotland and a rebellion called The Peasants' Revolt. The two countries resumed peaceful relations from 1389 to 1415.

Sixty years later, more than half of the ransom money had not been paid and France controlled most of Aquitaine again. In 1415, the English king, Henry V, revived his claim to the French throne and led an army into France. He was outmaneuvered and low on supplies when the two armies met at Agincourt.

King Henry V

The English army was three-quarters archers, and the larger French army was mounted knights and heavy footsoldiers. The battlefield was sodden with heavy rain and this slowed down the French charges. The English archers devastated both the French cavalry and infantry. Over forty percent of the nobility of France was killed in this one battle.

FRANCE ON THE RISE

England had defeated France, but could not hold on to its gains. Most French citizens rejected the idea of an English king. Inspired by Joan of Arc, who claimed she had received messages from God, the restored French army defeated the English at Orleans in 1429.

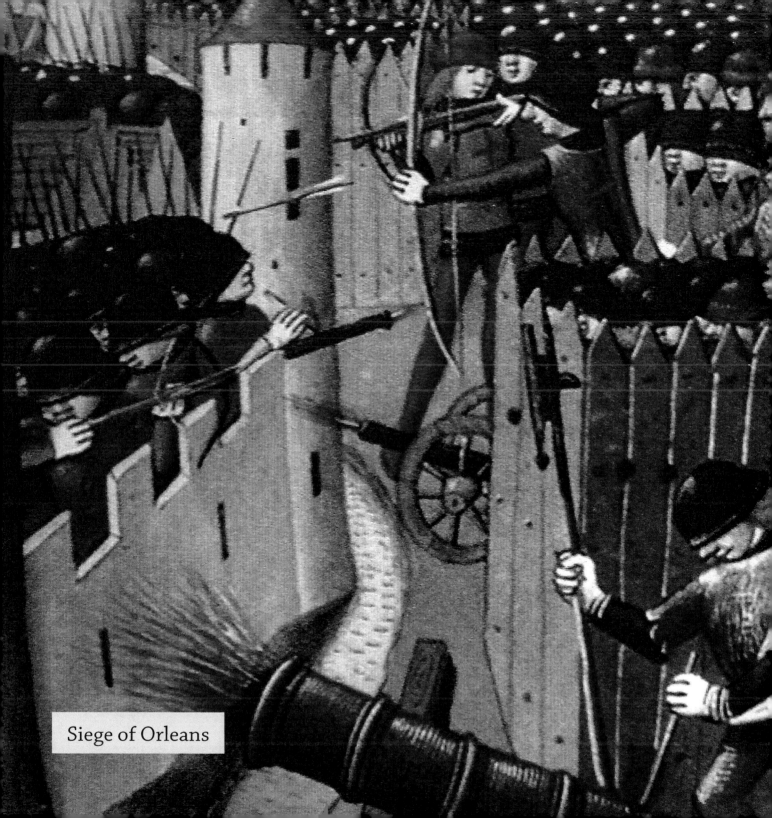

Siege of Orleans

Battle of Formigny Monument

The Duke of Burgundy, who had been an ally of England, changed sides to France in 1435 and reorganized the army. By 1441, the area around Paris (the "Ile-de-France") was back in French hands, and the French conquered Normandy in 1450 at the battle of Formigny.

THE END OF THE FIGHTING

The last great battle of the Hundred Years' War was at Castillon in 1453. The French victory there gave them control of all of Aquitaine. English territory in France, once so extensive, was now reduced to the city of Calais on the English Channel. England held on to Calais until 1558.

The Battle of Castillon

Finally, in 1475, England signed a treaty renouncing (again) any claim by the kings of England on the throne of France.

The pressure of war led to the development of weapons and tactics.

ARCHERS

England's decision to meet charges of cavalry with waves of arrows shot by longbows seems to have been a continuing surprise to the French.

LEADERSHIP

The English armies generally had a clearer command structure, with fewer disputes about who was in charge or what was to be done. France suffered from "leadership by committee", with many less-able nobles asserting hereditary rights to lead parts of the army as they thought best.

CANNON

The use of cannons on the battlefield and to attack cities began slowly as the early weapons were just not all that good. In 1431 the army of the duke of Burgundy fired over 400 cannonballs into a town during an attack and only managed to kill...a chicken!

Cannon

Bourg

However, within twenty years the power and effectiveness of cannons had improved so much that sometimes just having them on your side meant that the other side would surrender without a fight, which is what happened at Bourg in 1451.

At Formigny in 1450 field artillery contributed to the French victory. The French cavalry attacks failed to break the English line of archers. But when two cannon on carriages arrived and started to fire, they changed the momentum of the battle. They could fire from further away than the archers could, and weakened the English line, which fell back in the face of further attacks by reinforcements.

Battle of Formigny

War at Castillon

The final battle of the Hundred Years' War, at Castillon in 1453, was probably the first major battle where gunpowder artillery made the decisive difference. The battle marks the end of a century of conflict between France and England, and also the start of a new stage of war in Europe and the world.

TOTAL WAR

The standard for battles in the middle ages were for knights to fight against knights, and foot soldiers against foot soldiers, on battlefields chosen by agreement. Often the general population was little affected by the struggle going on just miles away.

Knights

However, in the Hundred Years' War, both sides identified the workers and peasants as valid targets. A dead peasant could neither grow crops nor pay taxes. This may have been the first European war in which general citizens were not ignored as non-combatants.

BOTH SIDES WON AND LOST

France and England were shaped in many ways by their long conflict, and by other events over that long century. France's population dropped to half its original size during the war, and England lost a third of its population, due to deaths from fighting and deaths from the plague and other illnesses.

The experience of the Hundred Years' War gave France a new respect for the importance of a competent, well-equipped, and well-led army. Losing the war gave England a stronger sense of itself as an island nation, somewhat removed from the concerns of the rest of Europe. This made it open to expanding into other areas, like India and the New World. Both countries gained a stronger national identity.

EUROPE'S FIGHTERS

The history of Europe has been made to a great extent by battles, victories, and losses. Read other Baby Professor books, like The Battles of Rome, How to Become a Knight, and Do All Knights Have Gallant Steeds?, to learn more about wars and fighters in Europe's past.

Visit

BABY PROFESSOR
EDUCATION KIDS

www.BabyProfessorBooks.com

to download Free Baby Professor eBooks
and view our catalog of new and exciting
Children's Books

Made in United States
North Haven, CT
27 November 2022

27397007R00038